GRIZZLY BEARS

John Woodward

Grolier
an imprint of

SCHOLASTIC

www.scholastic.com/librarypublishing

Published 2008 by Grolier
An imprint of Scholastic Library Publishing
Old Sherman Turnpike, Danbury,
Connecticut 06816

For The Brown Reference Group plc
Project Editor: Jolyon Goddard
Copy-editors: Lesley Ellis, Lisa Hughes,
    Wendy Horobin
Picture Researcher: Clare Newman
Designers: Jeni Child, Lynne Ross,
    Sarah Williams
Managing Editor: Bridget Giles

Volume ISBN-13: 978-0-7172-6255-7
Volume ISBN-10: 0-7172-6255-3

Nature's children. Set 2.
    p. cm.
 Includes bibliographical references and
index.
 ISBN-13: 978-0-7172-8081-0
 ISBN-10: 0-7172-8081-0
 1. Animals--Encyclopedias, Juvenile. 1.
 Grolier (Firm)
 QL49.N383 2007
 590--dc22
                        2007026928

Printed and bound in China

Contents

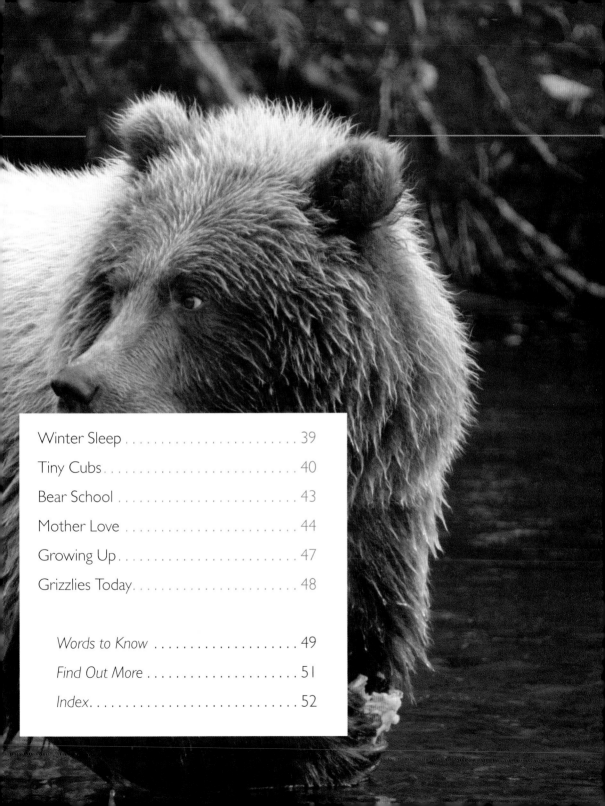

FACT FILE: Grizzly Bears

Class	Mammals (Mammalia)
Order	Carnivores (Carnivora)
Family	Bear family (Ursidae)
Genus	Brown, black, and polar bears (*Ursus*)
Species	Brown bear (*Ursus arctos*)
Subspecies	Grizzly bear (*Ursus arctos horribilis*)
World distribution	Alaska, western Canada, and the northern Rocky Mountains of the United States
Habitat	Forests and grasslands
Distinctive physical characteristics	Big, with strong shoulders, thick gray-flecked brown fur, and long, strong, curved claws
Habits	Lives alone or with young; has a territory; spends winter asleep in its den
Diet	Berries, nuts, seeds, roots, leafy plants, insects, fish, small mammals, and some big mammals

Introduction

The grizzly and its close relative the polar bear are the largest hunters in North America. A grizzly is strong enough to kill even its biggest **prey** with one swipe of its huge paw. But grizzlies don't just eat other animals. They eat plants and fruit, too. Grizzlies fatten up in fall and spend winter asleep, waiting for spring.

The word *grizzly* is not a misspelling of "grisly," which means scary. The bear actually takes its name from the word "**grizzled**," which describes hair that is flecked in silver and gray.

A grizzly bear crosses a stream.

Grizzlies
are a type of
brown bear.

Meet the Relatives

A grizzly bear is a subspecies of the **species** brown bear. There are three subspecies of brown bears: grizzlies, Kodiaks, and the European brown bear. Grizzlies live in northwestern North America. They are the only type of brown bear with grizzled fur. Kodiak bears are bigger and browner than grizzlies. They live on Kodiak, Afognak, and Shuyak Islands off the southern coast of Alaska. European brown bears live in Scandinavia, northern Russia, and Siberia. They also live in parts of southern and eastern Europe and central Asia.

The brown bear's closest relatives are the polar bear, which lives in the Arctic, and the American black bear, which lives in North America. The polar, brown, and black bears are so closely related that they can breed together. Though that usually happens only in zoos rather than in the wild. However, in 2006 a hunter in Canada shot a wild cross between a polar and grizzly bear, known as a "grolar" or "pizzly" bear.

Big and Furry

Grizzly bears can be massive. Some of the biggest males, called **boars**, grow to about 9 feet (2.7 m) long and weigh as much as 1,200 pounds (545 kg). Female grizzlies, or **sows**, can grow to almost the same length as males, but they are much lighter. Sows weigh up to 550 pounds (250 kg). The huge difference in weight is due to muscle—boars are very muscular and, therefore, extremely strong. In addition, a grizzly's weight changes greatly with the season: they put on a lot of extra weight in fall in order to survive the hardships of winter when food is difficult to come by.

Grizzlies look bigger than they really are because their fur is so long and thick. It is especially long around the neck and shoulders, where it forms a thick **mane**. Their fur can be any shade of brown, from pale blond to almost black. No matter what shade of brown, every hair is tipped, or frosted, with gray to give the fur its grizzled look.

The shoulders of an adult grizzly stand up to 5 feet (1.5 m) high.

9

A grizzly mother and her cub sit down in a mountain meadow.

Bear Country

Grizzlies used to live as far south as Mexico, but these southern bears disappeared in the 1970s. Today, grizzly bears are found only in Alaska, western Canada, and the northwestern United States.

Grizzlies like river valleys and grassy places. These regions provide the bears with the plants and animals, including fish, that they like to eat. They also live in forests and on mountain slopes. The bears often climb to regions where it is too high and too cold for trees to grow. They roam onto the half-frozen **tundra** on the shores of the Arctic Ocean. Their thick fur makes them well suited for these cold regions.

Walking Tall

Many animals such as dogs, cats, deer, and horses walk on their toes, which makes them look agile and graceful. But a bear walks with its feet flat on the ground, with its toes turned in. That makes it seem a bit clumsy.

Being flat-footed can be useful though. When a grizzly wants to sniff the air to locate the source of an interesting odor or reach up into trees, it can stand up on its back feet and even walk on them. The Native Americans called grizzlies "the beasts that walk like people." Although they can walk only a few steps in this upright position, it is very impressive! Once back on all fours, however, a grizzly bear can run at 36 miles per hour (58 km/h)—as fast as a horse—over a short distance. Grizzlies are even quick enough to chase and kill small deer.

A grizzly from
Utah stands on
its back legs and
sniffs the air.

One of the few times grizzlies gather is to catch salmon.

Strong Claws

A grizzly has five long, sharp, curved claws on each foot. They are extremely strong. The bear uses them for catching fish, killing small animals, and digging up the juicy roots of plants. Digging is hard work, but a grizzly bear has very big shoulder muscles that make the job easier. Throughout summer, all this digging wears the claws down and makes them blunt, but they grow back over the winter.

As a grizzly bear grows older, its claws change color. At first they are black with pale tips, but over the years they turn gray, just like the hair of older people. Eventually the claws may turn pure white.

Brown and Black

In parts of northwestern North America, grizzly bears and black bears make their homes in the same regions. The black bears always stay in the forests. But grizzlies often live in forests, too. If they meet, there is likely to be trouble. Grizzlies are much bigger and often kill black bears that wander onto their **territory**, especially young black bear cubs.

Luckily, black bears are expert tree climbers. Grizzlies, however, cannot climb trees. So if a black bear is chased by a big, fierce grizzly bear, it can escape by scrambling up the nearest tree. The grizzly might wait at the bottom for a long time. Eventually the grizzly gets bored and wanders off. The black bear can then make its getaway.

An American black bear escapes from danger in the branches of a tree. Unlike black bears, grizzlies cannot climb trees.

A grizzly finds a tree to scratch. Claw marks on the trunk warn other bears to keep away.

Home Range

For most of the year, a grizzly bear lives alone. Males especially do not like company. Each bear has a **home range** which covers 40 to 800 square miles (100–2000 sq km). At the center of this large area is the bear's territory, where it spends most of its time. This area is about 6 square miles (16 sq km). The bear marks the boundary of its territory by scratching marks with its claws on trees. Neighboring grizzly bears know that these marks mean "keep out." Any bear that ignores the marks risks being badly hurt in a fight.

Scent and Sound

A grizzly bear has small eyes. Its eyesight is not very good. A grizzly, much like a dog, lives in a world of scent and sound. Its long nose is packed with **sensors** that pick up the slightest trace of scent. The bear has a very good memory for different smells. That helps the grizzly know where it is in the dark—when it is most active—and which animals are around. The bear's keen sense of smell allows it to avoid enemies, such as other bears, wolves, and people, as well as track down food.

The grizzly also has very good hearing, even though its furry rounded ears look quite small. It can hear the slightest rustle or crack of a twig, often from far away. That is one reason why people rarely see grizzlies. They slip away when they hear humans coming and stay out of sight until they have gone.

Small eyes and a big nose indicate that the grizzly relies on smell rather than sight.

21

Grizzlies have a varied diet that includes grass.

Dinner Time

Although grizzly bears belong to a group of animals called **carnivores**, or meat eaters, they actually eat almost anything. Grizzlies feast on berries and other fruit, as well as nuts and seeds. They dig up fat juicy roots, and enjoy munching on tender young shoots. They also love honey. Grizzlies raid the hives of wild bees without worrying too much about the stings. They also dig grubs, mice, and ground squirrels out of their burrows, and catch fish. If given the chance, they will kill and eat bigger animals, such as mountain goats, elk, and moose.

Grizzlies use their keen sense of smell to find most of their food. They also have color vision, which helps them to pick out colorful ripe berries. Because they have an excellent memory, they know where they have found food before and at what time of year. That is a very helpful skill to have in the far north, where the amount of food available varies with the seasons.

All-purpose Teeth

Most carnivores have sharp teeth for slicing through meat. Carnivores do not have to chew, but rather swallow the meat in big chunks. For this reason, their chewing, or back, teeth are quite small. But a grizzly bear eats many plant foods that need a lot of chewing. Therefore, its back teeth are broad and flattened for crushing and grinding roots and leaves. It also has extra-strong jaw muscles for cracking nuts and other tough foods.

Since a grizzly bear also hunts, it has four long, sharp teeth at the front of its jaws for killing its prey. It also uses these teeth to break into rotten wood in order to find insects and to fight with other grizzly bears.

Hungry Hunter

Most of the animals that a grizzly catches are rats, mice, and ground squirrels. The bear digs them out of their burrows with its strong claws. But the grizzly also hunts bigger animals, such as deer and mountain sheep, chasing them with surprising speed. During early summer the grizzly can be a serious threat to young moose or caribou. Sometimes a hungry grizzly will kill domestic sheep or calves on **ranch** land.

If it has more meat than it can manage to eat all at once, a grizzly might drag the remains into the bushes. There, the bear hides the remains by covering them with branches. When the bear feels hungry again, it returns for a second helping—provided other animals have not already finished off the grizzly's kill.

A grizzly in Alaska eats
a freshly caught salmon.

Fishy Feast

The grizzly bears that live near the Pacific coasts of Alaska and Canada enjoy a treat in summer. Salmon swim upriver from the ocean to lay their eggs. The fish tire themselves out swimming against the current. That makes them easy to catch. The bears often just scoop them out of the water with their paws, carry them to the bank, and eat them.

The strongest grizzlies claim the best fishing places, warning off other bears with growls and threats. Younger bears often have to fish from more difficult spots or in a group. They sometimes have to jump right into the river to catch the salmon.

A grizzly's sharp
teeth quickly kill
a thrashing salmon.

A grizzly bear searches through garbage for food.

PREMIUM BANANAS

Leftovers

If a grizzly bear finds the body of a dead animal it will most likely eat it. This behavior is called **scavenging**, and it's a normal part of nature. Some bears scavenge leftover human food from garbage dumps near towns or campsites. And that can lead to trouble. If grizzlies come into close contact with people and cannot get away easily, the bears might attack. People can be badly injured or even killed, and the bears might get shot.

Between 1900 and 2002, there were 220 attacks by brown bears on humans reported in Alaska. In 45 of these attacks, the person was fatally injured. Attacks seem to be increasing, too, as humans encroach on the bears' habitats and compete with them for food. However, outside Alaska, bear attacks are much less common.

The Mating Season

Every other year in early summer, a female
grizzly seeks out a male to **mate** with, so she can
have cubs. The males in the area know when a
female is ready to mate from her scent. If two
males find her at the same time, they might fight
over her. The winner mates with the female and
stays for one, two, or sometimes three weeks.
During this time he makes sure that other males
keep away. The male then leaves. When the cubs
are born in late winter, the female raises them
on her own. If the male runs into the cubs later
in the year, he will have no idea that he is the
father of the cubs.

Two male grizzlies fight over a female grizzly. The winner will mate with the female.

When the weather gets colder, a grizzly's fur gets thicker.

Ready for Winter

In early fall, grizzly bears start to get ready for the long cold winter ahead. They eat greedily, making the most of all the berries, fruits, and nuts on the trees and bushes. The more they eat, the fatter they get. The fat forms a thick layer under their skin that keeps out the cold. The fat also stores food energy that the bears can use later. That allows them to stay in their **den** without eating during the coldest months.

Each bear also grows extra-thick fur to help keep it warm. This coat has two layers: **guard hairs** and underfur. Guard hairs are long and form the outer layer of hair. They cover the underfur and stop it from getting wet in the rain or snow or when the bear wades into a river. The underfur is woolly. It traps little pockets of air. The bear's body heat warms the pockets of air. The warm hairs then work in the same way as a thick blanket. The two layers of hairs keep the bear nice and warm throughout winter.

Snug Den

Some northern hunters, such as wolves, stay active throughout the year. But a grizzly bear cannot find enough food in winter. Without food, it has no energy, so it spends the coldest months asleep. As soon as food becomes scarce in late November, it starts looking for a snug, dry den where it can sleep without being disturbed. It might find a cave, or a hollow beneath a boulder or fallen tree. Often the bear has to use its strong claws to dig out a big enough hole. It then crawls in, gets comfortable, and waits for snow to hide the entrance. Eventually it falls asleep.

This grizzly is digging out a cozy den for itself.

Woken by warmer
weather, this bear
will take a short
walk and then go
back to sleep.

Winter Sleep

A grizzly might sleep anywhere from several weeks to six months in its winter den, depending on how harsh winter is. During the long sleep, the grizzly's body temperature drops slightly and its heartbeat and breathing slow down. The bear uses only a small amount of energy each day. That means the energy stored in its thick layer of fat is enough to keep it alive until spring. Even so, a grizzly may wake up on a sunny winter day, and stretch its legs outside its den. It then goes back to sleep until the weather is warmer.

Tiny Cubs

Female grizzly bears that mate in early summer have their cubs in midwinter in their dens. Each female may have up to four cubs, though two or three is more usual. The cubs are tiny, blind, and helpless when they are born. They need their big, furry mother to keep them warm. She feeds them on rich milk, and they grow quickly. By spring each cub weighs about 20 times as much as it did when it was born. Meanwhile their mother gets thinner and thinner. She eventually has to leave the den to find food.

This baby grizzly is
only ten days old.
Its eyes and ears
are still closed.

These young bears are learning to find food with their mother.

Bear School

Once the family has left the den, the cubs have
to learn to find their own food. They follow
their mother and try to copy what she does.
It's not easy because bears eat so many different
foods. There is s a lot to learn, and the cubs
often get confused. Little by little they find out
which foods are good to eat, and which are not.
They learn how to catch small animals such as
insects and mice, too. Their mother also teaches
them how to avoid enemies like wolves and
other bears. Big male grizzlies are especially
dangerous—even the cubs' own father is a threat!

Mother Love

A mother grizzly bear has no fear. She will threaten any animal that she thinks is a danger to her cubs, including other grizzlies that are bigger than she is. Most enemies will usually back off rather than risk a fight. When raising her cubs, a mother grizzly can be particularly dangerous to humans. People who come across grizzly bear cubs while trekking in the wild should move away slowly and quietly. The sow is always close by. She will see the hikers as a threat to her young. She is likely to attack anyone who gets too close to the cubs.

Grizzly bears are
shy and usually stay
away from people.

This young bear is now old enough to fend for itself.

Growing Up

Gradually the cubs learn to find their own food, and often go off to explore by themselves. But if frightened, they immediately run back to their mother. Bear cubs stay with their mother all through the entire winter following their birth. The family shares a big den and helps keep one another warm. But in spring the mother gets tough with her cubs. She forces them to leave home before she mates and starts another family.

The young bears are not entirely on their own, though. They have one another for company. Young bear cub siblings will stay together for at least another year. By the end of the following winter they may be ready to live by themselves. Bear cubs continue to grow for another ten years. Grizzlies start mating and having their own cubs between the ages of 4 and 6 years. Grizzly bears can live in the wild for more than 25 years.

Grizzlies Today

In 1900 there about 100,000 grizzlies in North America. With the loss of suitable habitat due to human settlements, mining, and road building, the number of grizzlies has now decreased to about 30,000. The vast majority of these bears live in Alaska and Canada. Only about 1,000 grizzlies live in the United States.

Grizzly bears are protected in most states. Hunting is still allowed in Alaska and Canada, however. Recently, the grizzlies in Yellowstone Park—an area that covers parts of Wyoming, Montana, and Idaho—have lost their protected status. That means that the bears—about 600 of them—might now be at risk of losing more of their habitat.

Words to Know

Boars Male bears.

Carnivores Animals or groups of animals that eat meat, such as bears, cats, dogs, weasels, raccoons, and hyenas.

Den The place where a grizzly bear spends the winter.

Grizzled A frosted effect on fur, created by each hair having a gray or white tip.

Guard hairs The long, stiff outer hairs of a bear's coat, which shed water and snow.

Home range The area that a bear wanders through during the year.

Mane A ruff of thick hair around an animal's neck and shoulders.

Mate To come together to produce young.

Prey	Animals that are hunted by other animals for food.
Ranch	An area of grassland used for raising cattle or sheep.
Scavenging	Feeding on dead animals or scraps.
Sensors	Special structures that allow an animal to sense things such as smells.
Species	The scientific term for animals of the same type that can breed together.
Sows	Female bears.
Territory	The area that an animal defends as its own private space.
Tundra	The cold, treeless lands that lie between the northern forests and the Arctic ice.

Find Out More

Books

Sartore, J. *Face to Face with Grizzlies*. Face to Face with Animals. Washington, DC: National Geographic Children's Books, 2007.

Thomas, I. *Polar Bear Vs. Grizzly Bear*. Animals Head to Head. Chicago, Illinois: Heinemann Library, 2006.

Web sites

Grizzly Bear
www.enchantedlearning.com/subjects/mammals/bear/Grizzlycoloring.shtml
Facts about grizzlies and a picture to print.

Wildcam Grizzlies
www9.nationalgeographic.com/ngm/wildcamgrizzlies/wildcam.html
Footage of grizzly bears in the wild.

Index